I Have a Question about Divorce

by the same authors

I Have a Question about Death
A Book for Children with Autism Spectrum
Disorder or Other Special Needs
Arlen Grad Gaines and Meredith Englander Polsky
ISBN 978 1 78592 750 8
eISBN 978 1 78450 545 5

of related interest

Divorce and the Special Needs Child
A Guide for Parents
Margaret "Pegi" Price
ISBN 978 1 84905 825 4
eISBN 978 0 85700 284 6

Great Answers to Difficult Questions about Divorce
What Children Need to Know
Fanny Cohen Harlem
ISBN 978 1 84310 672 2
eISBN 978 1 84642 818 0

**Helping Children with Autism Spectrum
Conditions through Everyday Transitions**
Small Changes—Big Challenges
John Smith, Jane Donlan and Bob Smith
ISBN 978 1 84905 275 7
eISBN 978 0 85700 572 4

You Make Your Parents Super Happy!
A book about parents separating
Richy K. Chandler
ISBN 978 1 78592 414 9
eISBN 978 1 78450 776 3

I Have a Question about Divorce

A Book for Children with Autism Spectrum Disorder or Other Special Needs

Arlen Grad Gaines and Meredith Englander Polsky

Jessica Kingsley Publishers
London and Philadelphia

First edition published in hardback in Great Britain in 2018 by Jessica Kingsley Publishers
This paperback edition published in Great Britain in 2023 by Jessica Kingsley Publishers
An imprint of Hodder & Stoughton Ltd
An Hachette UK Company

1

Copyright © Arlen Grad Gaines and Meredith Englander Polsky 2018, 2023
Images copyright © SymbolStix, LLC 2016. All rights reserved. Used with permission.
Front cover image source © SymbolStix, LLC 2016.

A CIP catalogue record for this title is available from the British Library
and the Library of Congress

ISBN 978 1 83997 755 8
eISBN 978 1 78450 734 3

Printed and bound in Great Britain by Ashford Colour Press

Jessica Kingsley Publishers' policy is to use papers that are natural, renewable
and recyclable products and made from wood grown in sustainable forests.
The logging and manufacturing processes are expected to conform to the
environmental regulations of the country of origin.

Jessica Kingsley Publishers
Carmelite House
50 Victoria Embankment
London EC4Y 0DZ

www.jkp.com

For Lucas, Jaycie, and Harlow

Acknowledgments

Our heartfelt thanks to Suzanne Adelman, Geoff Bernstein, Ellen Braaten, Barry Glassman, Rae Grad, Amy Guberman, Elaine Hall, Amanda Katz, Lori Kole, Karen Mann, Amanda Morin, Lindsey Nesbihal, Manny Schiffres, Joy Sexton, Katie Smeltz, Ray Smithers, Jennifer Whichard, and Jamell White.

We could not have written this book without the generosity of many parents who so graciously shared their stories and wisdom with us.

With much gratitude to Jessica Kingsley, Elen Griffiths, Simeon Hance, and the staff at Jessica Kingsley Publishers for their encouragement and guidance, and their passion for creating books that make a difference.

Thank you to our own families, who continue to support us in immeasurable ways.

Preface

Divorce is a difficult topic for any parent to explain to a child, perhaps even more so when the child has Autism Spectrum Disorder or other special needs. Many of these children process information in a concrete manner, prefer established routines, and need support understanding and interpreting emotions. We wrote *I Have a Question about Divorce* to provide a straightforward resource for children with special needs that takes these considerations into account and seeks to cover the wide range of questions that emerge as a child learns about divorce.

This book reflects real questions that children have asked as they are learning about their parents' decision to divorce. As an introduction to the topic, we hope that the book will lay the foundation for future conversations, whether about remarriage, step-siblings, or other life transitions that emerge.

We believe that special education is just really good education and hope that this book, and the strategies contained within, serves as a resource for *all* children. Similarly, gender-neutral language throughout the book aims to be inclusive of *all* families.

I Have a Question about Divorce consists of three components:

1. The complete story
Created with straightforward text and clear illustrations for children who process information best through words and pictures.

2. Short picture story
Designed for children who learn best through visual cues, and those who may want to re-read the story and think about it independently.

3. Suggestions for parents
Provides ideas for parents in supporting a child, particularly with special needs, through the process of divorce.

Hi! I'm a kid who likes a lot of things. I like sports, watching movies, and playing games.

I'm also a kid who likes to know what to expect each day. Most of the time that works out fine.

Most days are regular days. They go like this:

I wake up. I have breakfast. I brush my teeth and my hair. I get dressed for school and I walk to the bus.

I see my teachers and friends and work hard.
In the afternoon, I come home, do my homework,
and play at my house. I eat dinner, take a shower
(most nights!), and go to sleep.

Once in a while, though, something different happens and the day doesn't go the way I expect.

Today was one of those days. I learned something new. I learned that my parents are getting a divorce.

I really wasn't expecting that.

Now I have *a lot* of questions. I'm a kid who likes when there are answers to my questions. Today, I'm asking my questions and some of them have answers. But some of them don't.

"What does it mean that my parents are getting a divorce?"

That is my first question. It has an answer.

When people get divorced, it means that they are not married anymore. They don't love each other the way they did when they got married. Married people sign a paper that says they are married. If they get divorced, they sign a new paper that says they are not married.

"Are my parents getting a divorce from me?"

No. Divorce is only for adults. Parents can decide not to be married anymore, but they cannot divorce their children. They never stop loving their kids. That's the kind of love that doesn't end.

"I am also hearing a different word: separating. Is that the same thing as divorce?"

I learn that parents who are getting divorced get separated first. It's kind of like practicing for being divorced. Parents who are separated live *separately*, or apart, from each other. I guess that makes sense, but I can tell I'm going to have a lot more questions.

"Why are my parents getting divorced?" I want to know.

The adults talk about "grown-up" problems, and I think that means they're hard for kids to understand. I learn that this is a question that doesn't have an easy answer. There are lots of different reasons why parents get divorced.

"Who will be my parents now?"

I ask. I am getting worried.

Lots of things are changing, and that is hard. But this question has a really good answer. My parents will be my parents. That won't change at all!

"Will my parents always be divorced?"
I wonder.

I find out that my parents thought about this decision a lot, and that the plan is to stay divorced. I learn that a lot of other kids have divorced parents, too.

I start to wonder about where we're all going to live. It seems confusing. So I ask, "How will this work? Where will we live?"

I learn that different families do different things, but a lot of times there are two homes. One parent lives in one home, one parent lives in the other home, and I take turns living in both. I have my home with one parent, and I have my home with my other parent.

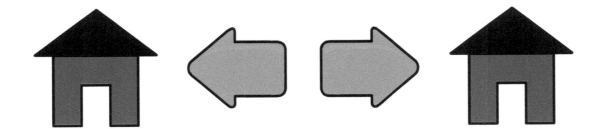

Even though that's a question with an answer, it still feels confusing. So I ask my next question: "What about my stuff? Where will my clothes be? What about my bed? And my toys?"

I find out that I will have what I need at each house. I will have clothes and toys at each house. Wherever I am, I'll have a bed that's just for me.

I can bring things back and forth that are special to me, like my favorite stuffed animal or my best fidget. I can use my backpack to carry my homework or the book that I'm reading. Maybe both homes will have movies and games, but they might be different. I can find a special quiet place at each home for when I want to take a break.

"What if I forget something that is special to me at one house, and I am already at my other house?"

That will happen sometimes. I don't really like that answer. But my parents will help me find a solution when I do forget something, and they will also help me remember things that are important.

I find out that even though some big things are happening, not *everything* is going to change.

This part is different for different kids. Some stay at the same school, and some kids change schools. Some kids go to activities in the same place, and other kids switch activities. But I learn that I won't have to be surprised. My parents will try to tell me about changes before they happen. That way I'll still know what to expect. I will still know what happens every day.

This is a lot of stuff to think about at one time. "What will divorce feel like?"

I learn that divorce can feel sad for kids and for grown-ups. I might cry. It's okay to cry when I feel sad. Even my parents might cry. Sometimes I might feel angry or confused. But I won't always feel those things.

It's okay if I want to talk about the divorce, and it's also okay if I don't.

Even though things are going to be different, lots of things will stay the same. I will have regular days again. I will still wake up, eat my breakfast, and go to school. My parents will still be my parents. We will still be a family—just a different kind of family. My parents will always love me. I will know what to expect every day. I will try to be flexible when things don't go exactly as planned.

I might think of more questions to ask. Now I know that a lot of my questions will have answers, but some of them won't.

Most days are regular days. Most days I know just what to expect. Today was not a regular day, but I learned a lot. Mostly I learned that asking questions really helps!

Short Picture Story:
I Have a Question about Divorce

On the pages that follow, you will see the same pictures used in the story along with shorter, more direct text. This is a tool for children who learn best through visual cues, and for children who might want to re-read and think about the story independently.

| Hi! | I like sports. | I like movies. | I like games. |

| Most days are the same. | I go to school. | I see my friends. | I come home at the end of the day. |

Today is different. My parents are getting divorced.

I have a lot of questions.

What does it mean when parents divorce?

They are not married anymore.

Are my parents getting a divorce from me?

No. Divorce is only for adults.

Is separating the same thing?

Parents get separated first.

Then they get divorced.

Why are my parents getting divorced?

There are lots of different reasons parents get divorced.

Who will be my parents?

My parents will be my parents.

Will my parents always be divorced?

The plan is to stay divorced.

Lots of kids have divorced parents.

Where will I live? This is different for different families. Often there are two homes—one for each parent. I will take turns at each home.

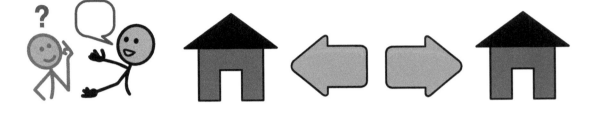

What about my stuff? I will have what I need at each house.

What if I forget something?

That will happen sometimes.

My parents will help me.

What about my schedule?

My parents will try to tell me about changes before they happen.

What will divorce feel like?

I might feel sad.

I might feel angry or confused.

I won't always feel those things.

Lots of things will stay the same.

My parents will still be my parents.

I will have regular days again.

Asking questions really helps!

The following are suggestions to support a child, particularly one with special needs, through the process of divorce.

Tailor the conversation to the child

Find ways to support the child based on his or her specific developmental needs. Remember that children will process the information in their own way and in their own time. Some may worry that they caused the divorce or wonder how they can "fix" it. Reassure the child that divorce is an adult decision; they are not responsible and are in no way to blame. Other children will not consider the concept of feeling at fault, so adults would not need to introduce this. Pay attention to their cues and tailor your response accordingly.

Acknowledge the practical implications

Children, both with and without special needs, often focus on themselves and may be less concerned about what is happening around them. Therefore, many children may concentrate on the practical aspects of the divorce experience rather than on the emotional. The child may perseverate on a seemingly irrelevant aspect of the experience, such as whether or not the new home will have internet access. Recognize that it is important to them, and support the child's immediate concerns.

Provide extra attention to transitions, consistency and routine

Many children with special needs have difficulty with changes in routine. Think about strategies that have worked well in other aspects of the child's life and utilize them to provide support. For example, a picture schedule, visual checklist, or calendar may help a child gain comfort with a new schedule. Knowing that routines and rules may vary between homes, try to maintain consistency as much as possible, allowing the child time to adjust to these new circumstances.

Provide sensory supports

As the child is processing and coping with the divorce, think about sensory-based strategies that have been comforting in the past. Consider having available a quiet space in each home, a pile of pillows to jump into, and sensory-friendly toys and fidgets.

Provide emotional guidance

Some children, including those with less verbal communication, may become withdrawn or irritable, experience behavioral changes, or show signs of regression as they experience their parents' divorce. Help them recognize their feelings, such as sadness, anger, or confusion, and provide messages of unconditional love. Partner with teachers, therapists, and others in the child's life to help support them during this time, assuring the child that divorce is not a secret.

Considerations for the parent

Whether or not a child has special needs, avoid talking negatively about the other parent in front of the child, and be sure not to use the child as a messenger. Consider ways to bolster your own support, by engaging, for example, with other parents, family members, friends, a religious community, a therapist, or support group.

Plan for continuity of care

As divorce planning proceeds, consider the specific social, emotional, and/or medical needs of the child, such as whether he or she may need medication management, therapies, medical equipment, or other factors that require continuity of care. When working through custody-related planning, find ways to delineate roles and the division of labor, and think about the schedule in ways that can accommodate the special needs of the child.

Consider future needs planning

A common concern of many parents of children with special needs is planning for such things as schooling, housing, and other long-term needs. This can get complicated in a divorce. Anticipating these factors may be helpful for parents in laying the foundation for a working relationship.

Arlen Grad Gaines is a licensed clinical social worker based in Maryland, USA. With a decade's experience in hospice social work, she has developed a specialization in supporting families who have children with special needs around the subject of grief and loss.

Meredith Englander Polsky has been working in social work and special education for more than 15 years and lives in Maryland, USA. She founded Matan, Inc. (www.matankids.org) in 2000, which has helped improve Jewish education around special needs for tens of thousands of families.